D1168967

Homeschooling Middle School with Powerful Purpose

How to Successfully Navigate 6th through 8th Grades

Lee Binz
The HomeScholar

First Printing, 2015

Printed in the United States of America

Cover Design by Robin Montoya
Edited by Kimberly Charron

ISBN: 1515358402
ISBN-13: 978-1515358404

Disclaimer: Parents assume full responsibility for the education of their children in accordance with state law. College requirements vary, so make sure to check with the colleges about specific requirements for homeschoolers. We offer no guarantees, written or implied, that the use of our products and services will result in college admissions or scholarship awards.

Homeschooling Middle School with Powerful Purpose

How to Successfully Navigate 6th through 8th Grades

What are Coffee Break Books?

Homeschooling Middle School with Powerful Purpose is part of The HomeScholar's Coffee Break Book series.

Designed especially for parents who don't want to spend hours and hours reading a 400-page book on homeschooling high school, each book combines Lee's practical and friendly approach with detailed, but easy-to-digest information, perfect to read over a cup of coffee at your favorite coffee shop!

Never overwhelming, always accessible and manageable, each book in the series will give parents the tools they need to tackle the tasks of homeschooling high school, one warm sip at a time.

Everything about these Coffee Break Books is designed to suggest simplicity, ease and comfort — from the size (fits in a purse), to the font and paragraph length (easy on the eyes), to the price (the same as a Starbucks Venti Triple Caramel Macchiato). Unlike a fancy coffee drink, however, these books are guilt-free pleasures you will want to enjoy again and again!

Table of Contents

Introduction

What is Middle School?

Many homeschool parents feel anxious about middle school. Often, this comes from memories about that time in their own lives. Before we started homeschooling, my husband and I considered homeschooling only middle school, because we remembered it being so difficult. I homeschooled my own two children and I know how scary it can be to homeschool middle school.

Middle school is, to be polite, an awkward time full of changing bodies and attitudes. Homeschool parents can find themselves suddenly staring across the breakfast table at strangers. Delightfully compliant children can suddenly act out like surly teens with attitude.

Thankfully, homeschoolers can shape and mold children through this process, even during bursts of hormonally charged awkwardness. You can ensure they learn appropriate behavior in the safety of your home.

Think about what your child looks like in middle school. Some children look as if they're eight years old, and some look as if they're 18 years old — it's different for every child. It's okay for them to look different ages in middle school and it's okay for them to be at different academic levels in middle school, too.

Defining Middle School

Grades seven and eight are usually considered middle school, when children are around age 12 to 14. In some areas, middle school will begin in grade six or end in grade nine. Your local middle schools may consist of grades six to eight, or grades seven to nine. In some locations, middle school is called junior high.

One Small Task

During the middle school grades, your job is to prepare your child for high school. That's all. One small task. I have great news. The way you prepare your child for high school is the same way you prepare them for success in life. Teach them to read fluently and write legibly. They will need to understand key math concepts so they can build on these skills in high school. Reading, writing, math, and attitude are the four cornerstones. Do what it takes to develop good study habits and a good work ethic.

Teach them to be independent, so they can eventually self-teach. At the same time, they will need to respect your leadership so they will complete assignments you give them. Teach them honesty, so they don't try to cheat or mislead you as they work independently. Keep their work in elementary school challenging so they know what it is like to *learn* instead of *know* new material. Make sure the work isn't overwhelmingly difficult so they don't learn to hate school.

Teach your child how to pace themselves and their work, so they don't suffer from burnout. Keeping a schedule may help, but others achieve this goal by limiting the time allotted for each homeschool task. Assign your child chores to help around the house, and make sure they know they are family members as well as students.

Chapter 1

The Purpose of Middle School

Purpose for Students

Middle school is the pause between elementary school and high school. Children learn at different rates — not only homeschoolers, *all* kids! The pause, middle school, gives slow or reluctant learners time to catch up before high school. At the same time, it gives quick and academically capable children a chance to continue learning at their level.

The first purpose of middle school is to give students in need some remedial help. Students below grade level in math can spend time focusing on math. They can use the time to reach grade level. The good news about middle school is that it's impossible for you to be behind. If your child is below grade level, then the purpose of middle school is to help them achieve grade level. You haven't done anything wrong and your child is exactly where they should be.

The second purpose is to give students who are ahead of grade level the chance to keep moving ahead, straight into high school level work. Children completing high school level work competently, using high school level material with good understanding, can obtain early high school credits on their transcripts. Algebra 1, biology, and foreign language are common high school level classes to teach in the middle school years.

Some children are right at grade level. Not all children require remedial work or are ready for advanced classes. Your child doesn't have to do remedial or high school work; you can have them do remedial work in certain areas, move ahead into high school work in other areas, and remain at grade level for the rest.

Your job is to teach your children at their level in each subject all the time. Your child might be on grade level for everything but math, or excel in foreign language but suffer in math, with other subjects right on target. The joy of homeschooling is being able to provide for your child's academic needs in *every* subject.

Middle school is a time for your children to learn something new. They need to learn how to learn, and should become increasingly independent and responsible. You want them to start taking ownership of their own education.

Parents often believe that on the first day of seventh grade their children will become independent and responsible. If you think so, you'll be sadly disappointed. Independence doesn't happen abruptly; it happens in fits and starts. Children will be independent one day and completely irresponsible the next. You need to be understanding. Like the hormones that affect a young person's mood from day-to-day, the same is true of their independence.

For boys and girls alike, independence and responsibility is not a straight line. It has its ups and downs. It's challenging; as a parent, you never know which kind of child you'll wake up to in the morning.

Purpose for Parents

The first purpose of middle school for parents is to spend time learning how to homeschool high school. This is your job. Home education is your chosen vocation. You have to invest. You need to include continuing education to avoid a crash and burn during the high school years. Learn what you need to know so you do not panic.

You're not only investing in college for your child, but also in yourself and your homeschool. Take classes about homeschooling high school and go on a business trip for homeschool parents — attend a homeschool convention. Take parent education training classes online, read books about high school, and buy books about college admission and scholarships. This will all help you afford college and help your child go on to life beyond homeschool — to college and career.

Middle school is the best time to learn about homeschooling high school. Identify your fears and educate yourself. If you're petrified of teaching algebra, you can educate yourself on algebra and the different curriculum available.

Learn more about high school while your child is in middle school. This is training time for you, not the final exam. This is your opportunity to get better at homeschooling.

Your job as the parent is not to panic. Fear of high school is usually what causes parents to quit homeschooling. Don't let fear rule your life. Become more educated so you can make informed decisions about your child's future, instead of fear-based decisions. Knowledge is power. Knowing more about middle school and high school will remove the fear so you can make an educated decision. Learn more to help you become more confident over time.

The second purpose for homeschool parents is to practice your record keeping skills. Begin to learn all about record keeping before your children are in high school. Keep great records and move forward with confidence. This is an opportunity for you to learn without any possibility of failure.

Practice keeping records as if your child was in high school. Begin working on a transcript and write course descriptions. Learn what type of attendance records homeschoolers must keep in your state. This will prevent panic when you face high school. For more information on record keeping, you might want to check out my book, *Setting the Records Straight*. It describes how to keep records and create transcripts and course descriptions.

Your most important purpose during middle school is to enjoy learning with your children. Enjoy this time with them while they're young. These are the last few years they will value your opinion and won't insist on having their own.

Value this time; learn to love and cherish it.

Your role as parent is to work yourself out of a job within the next six years. Train your children to become young adults who can live independently. It is a six-year process; you won't create an independent young adult instantaneously. From the time they're 12 until they're 18, it will take a lot of effort on your part.

Chapter 2

The Benefits of Middle School

The benefits of homeschooling don't run out when your child finishes elementary school. There are many benefits of homeschooling middle school.

Social Benefits

The best benefit of homeschooling middle school is the meaningful relationship it allows between parent and child. Parents who begin homeschooling at this age often experience a dramatic improvement in their relationship with their children.

Because homeschool parents spend time with their children, they can adapt, mold, and shape their behavior. Children even become easier to love over time. When you start homeschooling, your relationship smooths out as you figure out this new balance of normal in your home together. Children can develop their own opinions, and you can have high caliber discussions about current events, values, and faith. These discussions become foundational for children as they grow up.

Another benefit of homeschooling middle school is the quality socialization your child can experience. In public and private schools, children experience forced association based on age only. Real world socialization happens when your child is living with the family and socializing naturally in the community. As they experience quality socialization, it can build their self-esteem.

Home is also a safe and secure place to facilitate your child's learning, with no fear of bullying. Outside of school, your middle schooler can share friendships without anybody laughing or judging because they're too tall, short, fat, or scrawny.

In middle school, children try to decide who they're going to be. Are they going to be mean people, or are they going to be nice people? Before this age, kids generally want to be nice people. By the time they get into high school, they decide whether they want to be good or bad.

In middle school, children go back and forth and this is where the problem lies. From one day to the next, they don't know what to expect from each other. Their best friend today could be a mean girl tomorrow. It's such a confusing time and can be a horrible time in a child's life, when they're faced with other young people who haven't decided whether they're going to be bad or good.

One of the big benefits of homeschooling middle school is the opportunity to shape and mold your child's behavior on a day-to-day basis. Kids this age all have hormones rushing through their bodies. They can go from delightful to surly in 60 seconds or less. You can take the time to teach them it's okay for their hormones to rage on, but it's not okay to use rude language around their mother. You can help children understand the boundaries of appropriate behavior, no matter how they're feeling.

Some middle schoolers look as if they're still in elementary school. Other middle schoolers look like much older teens. One of my children was always at the smaller end of the scale and looked young for his age, because he was short. My other son was tall for his age and a bit more athletic, so he looked like a middle schooler. My children had a close friend who was tall and broad-shouldered; he looked like an 18-year-old from the time he was in middle school. These differences in physical maturity can be challenging.

The same thing is true of academics. Children have widely varying abilities in middle school. It's not your fault any more than it's your fault if puberty comes early. You haven't caused an early maturation rate since you cannot control it.

In the same way, your parenting isn't responsible for your child's incredible successes, either. Success has a lot to do with your child's physical maturity, just as the body and hormones direct the progress of physical growth and maturation.

Physical Benefits

You can adapt to the hormone changes your child is facing. Their changing body freaks them out and in this rush of hormones, their attitude can fluctuate. Physical and academic maturity will change. Maturation and intellectual rates vary. You can't do much to control it. At the same time, there's a lot you can do to support and encourage your child through these changes.

When you have a daughter who is physically mature, you can spend all the time it takes to teach her how to care of her own body. You can teach her about the beauty within and make sure boys and girls don't tease her because of her physical maturity. You can make sure she is safe at home (because an 18-year-old boy may think she's an 18-year-old girl).

As your less physically developed child matures, you can talk to them about how different maturity rates are normal. At home, they don't have to worry about changing for P.E. in front of 30 to 40 other teens and being teased because of their lack of physical maturity.

Character Benefits

You can instill your values and morals in your child to help them grow and mature, so they can influence the world rather than be influenced by the world. During this six-year period spanning middle school and high school, you try to raise an adult who can become salt and light and influence the world for the betterment of mankind. If you expose them to everything that happens on the evening news before they're mature enough, it can blow them out of the water.

This is becoming truer with the advent of social media. It seems as if the bad news and events of the world are so common and prevalent that teenagers believe they live in a scary world. Social media is not usually filled with high quality values. Middle school is such an important time for children to grow in their faith and understanding of right and wrong. You have less influence on them as they enter the high school years and start to form firm beliefs. Influence your child while you can.

You are able to provide an appropriate education based on your values and beliefs. At the same time, you can encourage the love of learning. Public education increasingly has an emphasis on inappropriate education that has nothing to do with literacy and everything to do with the general morals of society, that you may or may not agree with.

When you are in control of their education, you can make sure it's appropriate for your child. Appropriate education in middle school means you provide foundational knowledge they will build on over the four years of high school. You want them to have the understanding and literacy to move forward into the high school years.

Family Benefits

You will see gradual independence in your children. As they become more independent, you can give them the tools they need to succeed as an adult. They're not only home educating, they're home growing as well.

It's not as if you can drive up to your child with a truck full of adult tools and dump it all on them at once. Instead, supply the tools in a more methodical way, a bit at a time so they don't become overwhelmed with adult responsibilities.

Allow your child to practice responsibility in small doses.

Another family benefit is appreciation of being together. When you homeschool, you're at home together as a family more often. You can enjoy family time and have more time for fun during the day.

The middle school years can be challenging because it's often a time in our lives when we have less financial freedom. Our summer vacations were often stay-at-home vacations, but those are the times I remember best. Fun things you do together such as camping, touring around the city, dinners, and family discussions can all increase a bond between you that will grow into adulthood.

There is a time when children separate from family, become independent, and go on to become a member of a new family with their spouse. Take time to develop precious family memories, so after they have separated from your family they will remember the love of their parents and siblings. When they're ready, they will come back for a visit, be part of your family again, and go forward with a large family network in happiness for years to come.

Problem Solving Together

Another benefit of homeschooling middle school is the opportunity to solve problems together and face challenges head on. There are tough, ethical questions families face all the time. You'll see things on the news that are challenging to your faith, your values, and your beliefs.

When you homeschool middle school, you can work through these issues together. When your children struggle, act out, misbehave, or even experiment with drug or alcohol use, you can work through them at home together.

Parenting never gets easier; it becomes more challenging. But when you work through challenges as they occur, they don't pile up and cause stress. High school will go more smoothly. Your child will have already figured out some tough ethical challenges. When your child's friends ask about their thoughts on issues, they will have already thought them through and will have answers ready.

Chapter 3

How to Plan and Prepare for Success

Provide an organized study space with all necessary tools at hand. Have a place to keep papers — perhaps a notebook for each subject. Encourage your child to work with a schedule or assignment list and to use a calendar for assignments. When they have a regular time, place, and procedure for studying, children are more likely to take good study habits with them to college.

Show your child how to manage their assignments. It often works to do the "worst first." They can work on the most difficult or least enjoyable subjects first. It also helps to break big projects into smaller steps and estimate the time each step will take.

Four Keys to Organizing Your Middle School

1. Learn on Purpose Every Day

You want your child to learn on purpose every day. This does not mean knowing how to use formulas on a spreadsheet. It means your child is learning something they don't already know. Learning on purpose is easiest when using a challenging curriculum and taking challenging classes.

2. Use Challenging but Not Overwhelming Curriculum

Challenging means your child has to try. It does not mean overwhelming. Don't ask your child for too much. They cannot possibly succeed when you're asking for too much time or too much difficulty. Avoid overwhelming classes and curriculum so they can succeed.

3. Develop Good Habits

This can be a challenge for parents who feel they don't have good habits. You're trying to raise a responsible adult and even if you don't feel like one, you can still work to train your child to develop good habits. If you're not an organized person, this is a great opportunity for you and your child to learn to develop good habits together.

4. Give Your Child an Annual Assessment

An annual assessment is a requirement in many states. In some states, it's optional and parents can dismiss the idea of an annual test. I think an annual assessment can help you with your middle schooler in two distinct ways.

First, an annual assessment will help you know where your child is academically. Are they ahead? Are they behind? Is there a piece of their education missing that you need to know about?

Secondly, an annual assessment gives your child some practice with tests. Eventually, they will grow up and take an SAT test, ACT test, or a driver's test and you don't want them to freeze up and panic because of test anxiety. Giving your child a meaningful grade-level assessment once a year can often help you to understand your child, and help your child understand the test-taking process.

Scheduling and Time Management

In elementary school, homeschooling means encouraging your child to play, enjoy, and experience learning. When children get into middle school, you also want to give them an understanding of the adult world of scheduling and time management, letting them love learning at the same time. This is the time to teach, encourage, and practice time management and organization.

Organization skills do not happen magically. You can't flip a switch and make your seventh grader suddenly organized and able to wake up with the alarm clock. In fact, the opposite is true because a pre-teen's sleep needs are so great that it becomes difficult for them to wake up with an alarm clock.

Teach and practice time management and organization skills. Try different schedules and allow feedback from your child. It doesn't matter if they do math before noon or after noon. Schedule assignments and set aside a specific amount of time per subject.

Some moms are good at scheduling and know years in advance what they're going to work on. Other families can't possibly understand planning that far ahead, which is okay, too. They may simply decide to do math at nine and history at ten every morning. By allowing a certain amount of time per subject, they get the same amount of work done, and their children still get an education and can be equally successful.

When I homeschooled middle school, I tried a variety of different scheduling methods. I tried to schedule one-day-at-a-time. I also tried a weekly schedule. From there, we moved on to giving our kids an entire week at a glance. This gave them an open-ended schedule for the week. They learned quickly that they couldn't get all the work done if they put it off until Friday every week.

It doesn't matter what you choose. Find the schedule that fits you and your child best.

Teaching Study Skills

Help your children to understand time commitments to make sure expectations are reasonable while they balance school and friends.

Remind children that daily study is most effective. Help them avoid cramming for tests or writing papers at the last minute, as can sometimes happen in co-op and classroom settings.

Provide assignments so students can complete work on their own while learning time management skills. Give them one day at a time at first. Then start to give assignments one whole week at a time. Much later in high school, your child will be ready for long-term assignments, perhaps one month at a time.

A schedule can be helpful so the child will understand adult work, high school work, college work, and career work. They can get used to doing tasks that need to be completed within a set time frame.

Encourage them to use a calendar so they can track their assignments and activities. Some kids love calendars. Teach your kid how to use a calendar on purpose.

Help your child learn to finish assignments on time. At the same time, you do want to have a bit of flexibility. Schoolteachers also have flexibility and you should, too. Strike a balance; encourage children to finish assignments on time but be flexible if something comes up.

Teach your children the strategy of worst first and work first. Worst first means their weak area is the first thing they work on during the school day to get it out of the way. Work first means they do the work and then they can go out and play. This concept can help your child develop a strong work ethic and become a better worker in the real world.

Teach your child to take study breaks. I suggest about 30 to 50 minutes of study followed by a 10-minute break. This is even more important for active learners, young men, and athletes. Regular exercise breaks can help teenagers manage hormones.

It is unhealthy to sit at a computer all day. Children need to get up, stretch their legs and bodies, stretch their minds and stop thinking about work. It's like taking a deep cleansing breath or eating a cracker between samplings of cheese. Children need a break before they can move on.

Taking a break does not always come naturally to kids. They can be either a little lackadaisical and feel as if they will never get to their math assignment, or feel a sense of perfectionism or drive to finish it. There is a point of diminishing marginal return, especially with subjects such as math; a child can only handle so many math problems before the brain refuses to do math anymore. Make sure your child gets regular study breaks.

Do not allow your child to cram for tests or procrastinate and write papers at the last minute. It's something you have to teach conscientiously. When you homeschool, you don't see as much of a problem with cramming for tests, but it can occasionally happen if children take classes outside the home or in a co-op. Keep your focus on the purpose of homeschooling — to learn and enjoy it — not to cram for tests.

Teach your child to take tests calmly, without anxiety, for optimal performance. This can be challenging for some who have trouble settling down and facing situations calmly. Try to give them a calm, matter-of-fact attitude toward test taking.

It's much like teaching bravery. I taught my children bravery by explaining that bravery can involve crying; it's okay to cry when you're being brave. Being brave means doing what you need to do.

I encourage you to teach your children test taking the same way you teach your children about going to the doctor. It's not something to freak out over. There may be a moment of discomfort, but it will help in the long run. Middle school is the right time to teach this.

Work to get children to the point of independent study when they are able. It varies by subject and by child, and frankly, it varies by curriculum, too.

Six Pitfalls to Avoid

1. Don't Expect Instant Maturity

Some children look as if they're eight years old and others look as if they're 18. Don't expect them all to mature at the same time or act maturely at the same time—not even on a day-to-day basis.

2. Don't Expect Consistent Behavior

A middle schooler's moods and hormones are changing. Good moods and bad moods happen to all of us, so we shouldn't expect consistent behavior from our children. We want to shape and mold their behavior so they become more adult-like and able to modify their behaviors as adults do, no matter how they're feeling.

3. Don't Expect Learning Styles to Change

Some parents believe when their children hit seventh grade they should immediately take to textbooks like bees to honey. It doesn't work that way; their learning styles stay the same. Your active, wiggly boys will still be active, wiggly seventh and eighth graders. Shy girls will still be shy. Search for a curriculum that will allow your wiggly child to wiggle it out with math and your auditory learner to enjoy science or history.

4. Don't Expect Complete Independence

Children won't turn on their independence all of a sudden. That's not how it works. Teach your children independence and work yourself out of a job.

5. Don't Compare — Someone Will Get Hurt

Someone always gets hurt when parents get caught up in comparisons. Never is this more true than in middle school, when some children mature early and some late — few mature right "on time."

6. Don't Have Unreasonable Expectations

It's always a good idea to ask yourself whether you're doing too much or too little. Are your children working longer each day than you would be able to work? Are you expecting your child to be more responsible than you are?

Proceed at Your Child's Pace

Expect slow and gradual changes. Think about the difference between a newborn baby and a two-year-old. It didn't happen overnight; it took two years.

Expect your middle schooler to change in stops and starts, as a baby will roll over then seemingly do nothing for the longest time. All of a sudden, they go from crawling to walking, and the next day they're running.

Gradual changes will happen when you have a middle schooler, too. Suddenly they'll act responsibly for one thing, but won't be responsible for something else. You need to be patient. Proceed at your child's pace.

Preparation for Life

Homeschooling middle school is preparing children for life. Help your child be as prepared as possible so they can use all the gifts God has given them for the betterment of society.

Teach your children to read, write, and speak confidently. Teach them to do math quickly, accurately, and easily. This is your goal so your children are prepared for life.

Consider planning your middle school and high school courses. A rough draft with a five or six-year plan can eliminate some of the, "Oh, no! High school!" panic I sometimes see. Develop a plan that includes English, math, science, and social studies each year. Consider beginning foreign language study in middle school so your child can ease into it, allowing for plenty of time for the two to three years of foreign language many colleges require.

Chapter 4

Sensible Strategies for Getting Things Done

Middle school is the time to advance and expand your child's literacy. Literacy includes reading, writing, and math. Handwriting must be legible and they have to spell reasonably well or they will not be considered literate. When you see people in the store who can't count out their money, you consider them illiterate.

Your job is to advance and expand your child's literacy so when they become an adult, they are ready to be part of society. This happens at uneven rates.

One child may have extreme difficulties reading or even challenges writing three-letter words. Another child might read classic Jane Austen novels in middle school. Both children are normal. Try to move your child along the rungs of the ladder towards literacy, taking one step at a time and not making them jump to the top of an eight-foot ladder. They might come crashing down again and hurt themselves.

Reading, writing, and math are all pieces of literacy — they are core subjects. Social studies and science are also core classes. Beyond these core classes, you'll find foreign language, critical thinking, art, and Bible classes.

Create Good Habits

One of the best core strategies is to create good habits. Develop study skills and habits that will take your child on to high school and into adulthood. Work toward independent self-teaching, a little at a time.

For every 15-minute moment my children worked independently, I was so thrilled. These were my 15 minutes of peace — when I could get my laundry done. It starts small, with 15 minutes of independence at a time. It is gradual.

You are the person in charge of home education and your child needs to respect your leadership. They should complete assignments without complaint.

Teach your child to understand honesty so they never cheat or mislead. It is possible for homeschoolers to cheat; it's unusual, but it can happen. Check in on your child on a regular basis. It's difficult to catch cheating happening day-to-day. If you check in with your child with a morning meeting once a day or three to four times a week, you'll know if they're cheating — it will become obvious.

Good habits include doing chores. Young people are family members as well as students. Delegate some of the household chores to them. Each year, they can become more responsible, not only for homeschool tasks, but also for household chores.

A Wide Range of Normal

There's a wide range of normal in middle school. Expect a variety of abilities. There are superstar students. Some are extremely gifted or academically capable because they're driven. Other students have challenges in one area or multiple areas. Remember, there's nothing you can do wrong as a parent of a middle school child. Accept them where they are in their range of normal.

Remedial Learners

It can be stressful when you're faced with a child who is struggling to learn. A child's maturity level and learning ability varies. The brain may not be capable of tasks it hasn't developed the synapses for, such as diagramming sentences. The cause could also be a learning disability such as dyslexia.

First, focus on the different learning styles. See if you can meet your child's needs by adapting so they can learn in a way that makes more sense to them. For an auditory learner, start by assigning oral reports or having discussions instead of using written tests (especially if writing is a challenge). If your child finds reading difficult, use video or audio lessons.

In addition to discussions, consider reading aloud together; it's a common method used to help remedial learners in public and private schools. You can certainly do this, too. Give your child exactly what they need.

Allow movement while you teach. This is extremely helpful for wiggly children who need to move in order to learn. Research shows that a kinesthetic learner simply can't learn unless they're in motion. Don't sit your child at a desk without allowing them to tap their foot, tap their pencil, or move their arms and legs.

Any child will learn far less when forced to sit at a desk. Research shows children learn best through movement. Sometimes little things will increase your child's ability to learn. For some children, coloring while listening to a book read aloud or while watching a video can be helpful. For other children, sitting and bouncing on an exercise ball while working on their lessons or doing math problems helps them learn. When one of my children was in middle school, we let him jump on a little indoor trampoline while memorizing math facts. He absorbed them much better than he could have without movement.

Focus on getting information into and out of your student as easily as possible. Don't try to force a square peg into a round hole. Don't beat your child up about their weaknesses; teach to their strengths instead.

Get the information out as easily as possible. If your kid is a quick test-taker, tests might be useful. For some kids, discussion, projects, or making videos might be more efficient.

For remedial learners, it can be helpful to separate academic learning from social settings. If your child with severe dyslexia has to read aloud in a co-op class with other children, they may feel inadequate and incapable. Make sure friendship time is only for socializing and isn't mixed with academics.

You can also separate your child's learning disability from other subjects. Don't require reading in science or history for your child with dyslexia. You can read aloud to them, use audio books, and watch videos instead. Don't require your child with dysgraphia to write everything. Work on their area of disability, such as reading or writing, but don't work on it 24/7 in every subject; your child will get frustrated and end up hating to learn.

Work on challenging areas separately. Assign work at your child's level so they feel as if they're learning something new, but not so much that they become overwhelmed. Don't require too much.

You may need to seek help for your remedial learners. Challenges will often make themselves known when a child is in middle school. The first place you can look for help is your pediatrician. Sometimes it's as easy as going to an eye doctor. Many children seem to have a learning disability but all they need is glasses.

Attend homeschool conventions and try to find a local learning specialist. If you can't go to a convention, check out the convention website to see if any specialists attended and look up their contact information.

Chapter 5

Teaching Middle School English

In middle school, there is a wide range of normal. Your job is to meet your child at their level. When planning middle school courses, consider what you need to teach and how you can teach your eager or remedial learner. Keep each class at your child's ability level. Do not panic if your child is grade levels behind because that's what middle school is for — it's a time to remediate or accelerate.

Reading and writing make up the cornerstone of literacy and the ability to learn. Some kids don't need to be encouraged. Other kids need you to be conscientious about how you encourage reading.

How can you encourage middle schoolers to read? Let me count the ways! Encouraging reading can be a fun way to help children love learning. When reading is enjoyable, children see homeschooling as a fun educational option, not a chore forced on them by a taskmaster. Learn to make reading fun with these seven easy-to-implement ideas.

Seven Ways to Encourage Reading in Middle School

1. Create a Cozy Corner

In my homeschool, the cozy corner was any place our dog was hiding. Behind a couch or in the sun's rays, reading with a pet increases a sense of coziness, which children learn to associate with reading. You can supply pillows or blankets, and some parents create a corner near a bookshelf filled with fun and age-appropriate books.

You could create a cozy corner outside for a wiggly child. Put up a hammock in the corner of your yard or under a cover on your deck, so they can rock back and forth as they read. A rocking chair may also be helpful for kinesthetic learners who need to move as they read.

2. Design a Bedroom Paradise

As children get older, they may eschew their reading corner and spend more time in their room. You can create a bedroom atmosphere and routine that encourages independent reading.

Remove technology from their room first, so they read instead of playing online. Set up bedtime reading boundaries and a lights-out time. Pick up a fun or stylish reading light or headlamp for your child. Then, your child can read until they get sleepy and turn off the light without getting out of bed. Avoid letting them read using digital devices because it can negatively affect their sleep quality.

3. Provide a Yummy Treat

Some adults (like me!) love to enjoy their coffee while reading the paper each morning and other adults love to read a novel while sipping tea. Your teens can enjoy this same cozy yumminess. Provide cocoa or cookies to keep it simple or go all out and create a classic teatime, like the Tuesday Teatime suggested by Brave Writer, incorporating discussion and poetry with your treats. Sip tea or milk from fancy cups and saucers for your special teatime.

4. Increase Fluency with Fluff

Once your children learn how to read, the next step is increasing their vocabulary, speed, and fluency. Although reading challenging books helps increase vocabulary best, you may need to go in the other direction to help kids read quickly. You can increase speed and fluency by letting them read below their ability level.

I know my children may have spent too much time reading *Calvin and Hobbes* comic books, but the comics did teach them to read quickly. Be careful to preview the comics you provide, because they have changed over the past few years. You can use higher quality literature too, of course — books below their reading level. As reading becomes easier, they will read more quickly and become more confident.

5. Focus on Discussion, Not Confrontation

It's possible to beat the love of reading right out of a child if you analyze and dissect each piece of literature. It's not necessary or recommended to do literary analysis for every piece of literature they read.

Encourage reading for pleasure by avoiding comprehension worksheets when possible. Instead of asking test-like questions, occasionally engage in an open-ended discussion about the merits of the book and share feelings about it together. Constant literary analysis can cause children to think, "This must be school" instead of, "I love to read."

6. Brainstorm Tie-in Activities

Instead of formal analysis, you can substitute more enjoyable activities. Play games that relate to the book. Your child can even act out books using puppets or their Lego figures. Do a simple online search for great activities to study classic books. You can find recipes to bake, field trip suggestions, hands-on crafts, and movie suggestions.

Some families get together for a book club. It can be kept simple, with each child sharing a brief oral presentation about why they liked the book (or didn't) and why others should read it (or not). Sure, it's public speaking, but you can also make it enjoyable for children who simply want to get together for fun and treats.

When I was homeschooling, we gathered at a pizza place. After each child spoke, they received a gift certificate for a personal size pizza. My children were highly motivated by pizza, and it was a big success for our whole homeschool support group.

7. Avoid Reading the Wrong Books

Provide real books (not *school reading books*) with quality writing and great story lines. Some children say they don't like to read. They may feel this way because they read the wrong books! Try to find books that interest them with topics on their passionate subjects.

Branch out into different genres of fiction and non-fiction. Consider magazines, non-fiction on topics they engage in for delight directed learning, or even classic graphic novels, such as *Tintin in Tibet*. Anything that encourages them to read is a good idea. Enjoyable reading will make other reading easier for them. I know, you don't want them to read non-fiction and graphic novels exclusively, but providing a wide array of books will help each child find enjoyment in reading.

What to Avoid

Avoid making your child read a book and then automatically giving them a quiz on it. You can have a discussion instead, especially if you read the books in advance yourself. Enjoy a casual conversation. Consider assigning oral presentations that include discussion instead of confrontation.

Avoid book reports when possible. They don't have to be assigned for every book read. If your child is a prolific reader, this would mean too many book reports! One to five book reports a year is probably reasonable for most kids.

Avoid tests when possible. Ruth Beechick wrote in her book, *Yes, You Can Homeschool Independently for Grades 4-8*, that a test measures what a child does not know. A test includes questions somebody else came up with, and measures whether your child knows the answers. But there could be fifty questions not included on the test that your child does know the answers to. While testing measures what your child does not know; discussion can show you what your child does know.

It's also important to avoid schoolbooks. High quality authors do not write grade level school readers; educators who may not even write well are the authors. They meet public school standards and public school needs. When you choose quality literature instead (award winning books for example), you know they are well written.

One study compared a grade-level reader to a Newberry Medal winner. They opened to a random page in each book. In the grade level reader, they circled all the passive verbs, which signify weak writing (such as the word "was"). They found none in the Newbery Medal winner. They circled many passive verbs in the reader. In general, you want to expose your child to quality literature.

It's helpful to provide books in a variety of genres. There are many to choose from: mystery books, historical fiction, fantasy novels, action novels, and more!

Keep in mind that your child may like completely different books than you do. I don't like reading C.S. Lewis' *The Lion, the Witch, and the Wardrobe* or J.R.R. Tolkien's *The Hobbit*. My children loved these books and couldn't get enough of them.

Solutions for Remedial Readers

Competence and confidence is the goal. Your child should feel they are capable of reading well. Sometimes you have to avoid books that reinforce feelings of inadequacy. Avoid books at their grade level if the ability level isn't quite there.

Some kids in middle school read Jane Austen books, but this does not mean your child should. Your child may not be ready for these huge books. Reading difficult books beyond their ability can make your child feel inadequate.

Help increase their reading speed by allowing them to read some fluff. As I mentioned, I let my children read *Calvin and Hobbes* comics. They laughed right through them. I knew they had great reading comprehension skills because they laughed at the appropriate times. One of my friends has severe dyslexia and he always read "Popular Mechanics" magazines. His vocabulary and reading speed increased, even though his mom couldn't talk him into reading a novel.

An easy way to get started is to read the first three chapters of a book aloud to your child. This introduces your child to the vocabulary the author uses and gives them an understanding of the character and tone. Your child will also be eager to keep reading to see what happens after chapter three. Starting a book can be scary for a remedial reader. If you start the book for them by reading the first three chapters aloud, you can help them be successful.

If you have a reluctant reader, choose shorter classics. They can read a book in a week and only you know it was half the size of other books. For a dyslexic child, include audio books so they can follow along. For a kinesthetic learner, it can be extremely helpful to find books with an active main character. One high school reading example with an active main character is *The Adventures of Tom Sawyer*.

Writing

Provide daily writing practice. This can be as simple as putting pen to paper or typing on the computer, every day. Make sure you cover penmanship and your child's penmanship is legible. It doesn't have to be a specific style of penmanship, simply legible so others can read it.

You may want to include narration as a writing exercise in your English class. Have your child explain anything they read in their own words. You might have your child read a section of the book and then write out a narration for you. They will explain it in their own words so you can tell what they understood in the passage.

Consider including dictation as well. I found it extremely helpful, especially when I got to the point of teaching punctuation and style. I selected sentences or paragraphs from the quality literature we read. Then I read the section aloud to my children and they wrote it down. I read slowly and they transcribed it with the proper punctuation, grammar, and spelling. It gave them an understanding of what quality literature looked like on a paper.

Spelling and Grammar

Include vocabulary games to help expand your child's vocabulary. For spelling, I often recommend Spelling Power. It covers second through twelfth grades, so you only have to buy a spelling program once. Toward the back of the Spelling Power book, you can find spelling games to play for every learning style. For your kinesthetic learner, you'll find game ideas such as "write one word to fill up your entire white board" and "write one spelling word with shaving cream on a cookie sheet."

Kinesthetic learners need to move large muscle groups. Moving their fingers doesn't count — they have to move the whole arm. This is why sidewalk chalk or spray painting with water colors can be much better spelling activities than simply writing the word a hundred times on a piece of paper.

Some homeschoolers think diagramming sentences is important, but it's optional. It's not an activity included in most public and private schools. Many homeschoolers include it, but I don't want you to feel as if it's necessary.

Covering grammar every year is also optional. Middle school is a great time to teach grammar, but it often takes only one year. You don't need to return to it repeatedly. If you have a kinesthetic learner, I recommend a grammar program called Winston Grammar. It teaches grammar through moving pieces of paper around the table.

Chapter 6

Middle School Reading List

Sometimes it's hard to find good books for your middle schooler. If you have a reluctant reader, focus on short, classic books. For kinesthetic learners, focus on books with active main characters. If you have voracious readers, feed their book hunger with quality literature instead of junk. My kids were in this category and they read like crazy! Once they read one of the Little House books, I had them read the *whole* series. In our family, a homeschooling snapshot looked like a boy reading a good book while lying on top of a dog.

For moody children, avoid dark

characters or themes and locate uplifting books with heroes and over-comers.

Middle school reading lists have become darker in our current educational system. For a fascinating comparison, read the article, "Middle School Reading Lists 100 Years Ago vs. Today" at www.intellectualtakeout.org/blog/middl e-school-reading-lists-100-years-ago-vs-today. One resource that helped us choose books was *The Read Aloud Handbook*, by Jim Trelease. If you need help finding great books for high school kids or for kids advanced beyond their years, look over my "College Bound Reading List" on The HomeScholar website for inspiration!

This book list is based on commonly recommended books for middle school students, heavily influenced by the reading we have done with our own children. If you are not familiar with something on this list, please review the book first. It's been a long time since I read them myself, as the parent of a middle school student, and only you know your child's maturity level.

Word of caution: All families are different and must decide their own standards for the books their children read. Parents assume all responsibility for their children's education. If you are not familiar with something on this list, please review the book first.

Below are some great books for middle schoolers, age 11 to 13. For a printable and clickable reading list, check out "7 Ways to Encourage Reading in Middle School Reading" on The HomeScholar website.

- Adams, Richard *Watership Down*

- Alcott, Louisa May *An Old Fashioned Girl*

- Alcott, Louisa May *Little Women*

- Alexander, Lloyd *Prydain*

Chronicles

- Angleberger, Tom *Origami Yoda Book Series*

- Auer, Hope *A Cry From Egypt*

- Auxier, Jonathan *The Night Gardener*

- Babbit, Natalie *Tuck Everlasting*

- Barrie, J.M. *Peter Pan*

- Batson, Thomas Wayne *The Door Within* series (Christian allegory)

- Bendick, Jeanne *Galen and the Gateway to Medicine*

- Bendick, Jeanne *Galen Archimedes and the Door of Science*

- Berquist, Laura M. *The Harp and the Laurel Wreath*

- Black, Chuck *The Kingdom Series* (6 books)

- Blackmore, R.D. *Lorna Doone*

- Blackwood, Gary *The Shakespeare Stealer*

- Bolt, Robert *A Man for All Seasons*

- Bradley, Alan *Flavia de Luce* series

- Bunyan, John *Pilgrim's Progress*

- Burnett, Frances Hodgson *The Secret Garden*

- Carroll, Lewis *Alice in Wonderland*

- Carroll, Lewis *Through the Looking Glass*

- Cather, Willa *My Ántonia*

- Chesterton, G.K. *The Ballad of the White Horse*

- Cody, Matthew *Powerless*

- Cohen, Barbara *Seven Daughters and Seven Sons*

- Collier, James Lincoln *My Brother Sam Is Dead*

- Cummins, Maria Susanna and Baym, Nina *The Lamplighter*

- Cushman, Karen *Catherine, Called Birdie*

- Dagherty, James *The Magna Charta*

- Dashner, James *The Maze Runner* series

- Decamillo, Kate *Tiger Rising*

- Defoe, Daniel *Robinson Crusoe*

- Di Angeli, Marguerite *The Door in the Wall*

- Dickens, Charles *A Christmas Carol*

- Doyle, Arthur Conan *The*

Redheaded League

- Duprau, Jeanne *The Book of Ember* series

- Ellis, Deborah *The Breadwinner* (3 book series)

- Farley, Walter *The Black Stallion* series

- Fitzgerald, Jon D. The Great Brain

- Fletcher, Susan *The Shadow Spinner*

- Forbes, Esther *Johnny Tremain*

- Frank, Anne *Diary of a Young Girl*

- Freedman, Russell *Freedom Walkers: The Story of the Montgomery Bus Boycott*

- George, Elizabeth *The Witch of Blackbird Pond*

- George, Jean Craighead *My Side*

of the Mountain

- George, Jean Craighead *Tree Castle Island*

- Golding, William *Lord of the Flies*

- Gipson, Fred *Old Yeller*

- Graham, Kenneth *The Wind in the Willows*

- Hale, Shannon *The Goose Girl*

- Henty, G.A, *Freedom's Cause*

- Holling, Clancy *Paddle to the Sea*

- Hunt, Irene *Across Five Aprils*

- Jacques, Brian *Redwall Series*

- Jenkins, Jerry B. and LaHaye, Tim *Left Behind: The Kids* series

- Jewett, Eleanore M. *The Hidden Treasure of Glaston*

- Johnson, Lois W. *The Viking Quest* series

- Juster, Norton *The Phantom Tollbooth*

- Keith, Harold *Rifles for Watie*

- Kipling, Rudyard *Captain Courageous*

- Kipling, Rudyard *The Jungle Book*

- Konigsburg, E.L. *The Mixed Up Files of Mrs. Basil E. Frankweiler*

- L'engle, Madeleine *A Wrinkle in Time series*

- Lawrence, Caroline *Roman Mystery Series*

- Lee, Harper *To Kill a Mockingbird*

- Lewis, C.S. *The Chronicles of Narnia*

- Lindgren, Astrid *Pippi Longstocking*

- London, Jack *Call of the Wild*

- London, Jack *White Fang*

- Lowry, Lois *The Giver*

- Lowry, Lois *Number the Stars*

- MacDonald, George *The Princess and the Goblin*

- MacLachlan, Patricia *Sarah Plain and Tall*

- McAllister, M.I. *The Mistmantle Chronicles*

- McCaffrey, Black *Horses for the King*

- McGraw, Eloise Jarvis *The Golden Goblet*

- Montgomery, Lucy *Anne of Green Gables* series

- Moody, Ralph *The Dry Divide*

- Morris, Gerald *The Squire's Tale*

- Mull, Brandon and Dorman,

Brandon *The Fablehaven* series

- Myers, Walter Dean and Miles, Bill *The Harlem Hellfighters*

- Naylor, Phyllis Reynolds *Shiloh*

- Orwell, George *1984*

- Orwell, George *Animal Farm*

- Paterson, Katherine *Bridge to Terabithia*

- Paulsen, Gary *Hatchet*

- Pearson, Ridley *The Kingdom Keepers: Disney After Dark*

- Peretti, Frank E. *The Cooper Kids Adventure* series

- Polland, Madeleine *Beorn the Proud*

- Pope, Elizabeth Marie *The Sherwood Ring*

- Pyle, Howard *Men of Iron*

- Pyle, Howard *The Story of King Arthur and His Knights*

- Pyle, Howard *Otto of the Silver Hand*

- Pyle, Howard and McKowen, Scott *The Merry Adventures of Robin Hood*

- Rawlings, Marjorie Kinnan *The Yearling*

- Rawls, Wilson *Where the Red Fern Grows*

- Robinson, Barbara *The Best Christmas Pageant Ever*

- Rogers, Jonathan *The Wilderking Trilogy*

- Sewell, Anna *Black Beauty*

- Shafer, Ruth *Jashub's Journal*

- Speare, Elizabeth George *The Bronze Bow*

- Stewart, Trenton Lee *The Mysterious Benedict Society*

- Stevenson, Robert Louis *The Black Arrow*

- Stevenson, Robert Louis *Kidnapped*

- Stevenson, Robert Louis *Treasure Island*

- Sutcliff, Rosemary *The Roman Britain* trilogy (*The Eagle of the Ninth*)

- Thom, James Alexander *Follow the River*

- Tolkien, J.R.R. *The Hobbit*

- Twain, Mark *Huckleberry Finn*

- Twain, Mark *The Adventures of Tom Sawyer*

- van Stockum, Hilda *The Winged Watchman*

- Verne, Jules *Twenty Thousand Leagues Under the Sea*

- Verne, Jules *Around the World in Eighty Days*

- von Le Ford, Gertrude *The Song at the Scaffold*

- Wallace, Lew *Ben-Hur*

- Warner, Gertrude Chandler *The Box Car Children* series

- Washington, Booker T. *Up from Slavery*

- White, T.H. *The Sword in the Stone*

- Wibberley, Leonard *John Treegate* series

- Wilder, Laura Ingalls *The Little House* series

- Willard, Barbara *Augustine Came to Kent*

- Williams, Sarah DeFord *The Palace Beautiful*

- Williamson, Joanne *The Hittite Warrior*

- Williamson, Joanne *The God King*

- Wright, Harold Bell *That Printer of Udell's*

- Wyss, Johan Rudolf *Swiss Family Robinson*

- Verne, Jules *20,000 Leagues Under the Sea*

Chapter 7

Teaching Middle School Math and Science

Math

Practice math every day. Your goal is mastery but not perfection. Everybody makes math mistakes from time to time. Don't expect your child to be perfect, but you do want them to understand math.

I encourage you to include math games for fun in your homeschool. My favorite math games book for this age is *Family Math: The Middle School Years*. It includes games for learning about algebra concepts.

You can also incorporate more fun with math by using readers. The www.LivingMath.net website lists readers to help reinforce math concepts for kids who love to read. These books also work to encourage reading for kids who love math.

Math is often a scary subject for parents. This may be the first subject you find yourself turning to video tutorials. When this happens, don't panic — everybody gets to the place where they can't cope with math anymore. Remind yourself that this is part of teaching your children to learn independently. Using video tutorials is a good step.

When you decide to use a tutorial, incorporate student preferences in your choice of curriculum. Their preferences will astound and amaze you. I was quite surprised at the math book my children chose. I like math books with pictures, but they didn't. The same is true of video tutorials. Some kids have strong feelings about how the teacher looks, for instance. Make sure you view a sample tutorial with your child before making a purchase.

It is possible for your child to earn early high school math credits. If your child takes Algebra 1 or higher level math in middle school, these credits can go on the high school transcript.

Science

In middle school, your goal is to make science fun. You want to encourage a love of learning and get your child excited about science. Encourage curiosity so they can pick up a textbook and be excited about science in high school. Instead of using textbooks in middle school, you can focus on unit studies. You can also incorporate activities such as looking through a microscope, dissecting owl pellets, and visiting aquariums or marine museums.

Usually middle school science is a survey of science disciplines: a bit of physics, chemistry, biology, and earth science. Your child can earn early high school credits for science as well. If your child works on high school level science, you can include it on the high school transcript.

Chapter 8

Teaching Other Middle School Subjects

Social Studies

Social studies is an important subject to teach every year. It can include history, geography, government, society, and current events.

Make social studies fun. Don't include a textbook unless you want to. Enjoy making projects, crafts, and food with your child. Visit museums, and go on field trips. Your child can also learn through stories, DVDs, CDs, novels, biographies, and literature. Use timelines and do some mapping.

With social studies, your goal is to build a baseline of information. By the time your child starts high school and learns about World War I, they will know it came after George Washington in the timeline.

Foreign Language

Before beginning foreign language study, start with some pre-language supplements to make learning a foreign language easier. Learn Latin and Greek roots. The easiest way to learn is by playing a game called Rummy Roots. It's a fun game much like Go Fish. Your child will become familiar with the meanings of English prefixes and suffixes that came from Latin and Greek. It's a great way to dip your child's toe into a foreign language.

Some homeschoolers start with Latin as their first foreign language. It can be helpful because many European languages are rooted in Latin. By learning Latin first, you make it easier for your child to learn other languages. It's one of the reasons we started Latin in middle school and then learned French when my children where in high school. The Latin study made it much easier to learn French.

When choosing a foreign language, consider that it's easiest to teach one that's familiar. Even a bit of familiarity can help.

Foreign language studies can include reading, writing, speaking, and listening to the language. Studying the culture and geography is also important. Learn the countries and cultures that speak the language. Studying the culture can make learning fun. When I was in school, we made crepes in French class.

If your child uses a standard high school curriculum, you can count it as an early high school credit in foreign language on the transcript.

Physical Education

P.E. can mean physical education, physical exercise, or a combination of the two. The education portion might include teaching your child how important it is to take care of their body. The exercise portion can include anything your child does that breaks a sweat. The goal of P.E. is both fitness and fun. Teach them fitness is fun because exercise is fun.

Remember that middle schoolers face huge body changes. Make sure you cover health in your P.E. class. I recommend *Total Health* by Susan Boe. Her book was written for Christian schools about 20 years ago, however, so the information does not include the unusual challenges young children face today. Whatever books you choose, it's important to cover health and children's changing bodies.

Make sure you also discuss purity and relationships. Then you can go into the high school years knowing you've had the important discussions about health, sexual purity, and relationships.

It's also important to cover nutrition because your children are going through growth spurts. During these growth spurts, they often choose to eat as much junk food as humanly possible. You need to teach them about nutrition so they don't rely on junk food as their sole source of calories. Teach them good habits.

Many experts agree it's important that teenage avoid diets. Diet should not be a word used at home because of the problems with how children view their bodies. Their perception of their bodies is in flux when they're preteens and teenagers.

It's important to limit technology for overall fitness. Children are much more likely to use technology than play on their skateboards or with a basketball. You have to limit technology to a reasonable amount so your child gets the chance to go outside and play. Limit your child's technology use so their body can develop normally.

Emphasize personal fitness and having fun. Find a balance between fun and personal safety. Sometimes it's tempting to be too careful and prevent your child from going outside to play, but children need to learn to move their bodies and exercise for fun.

Fine Art

The fine arts include music, art, theater, and dance. You can expose your child to one (or more if you can) of the fine arts. Encourage personal expression in your child's artistic development. The arts can be hands-on subjects, with no tests, no curriculum, and including play when possible.

Art is a weak area for me personally, so I did use a curriculum. For other families, art is a natural part of life. Art does not involve any learning challenges. Have fun by experiencing art together. Your goal is to encourage natural ability, exposing your child to art, music, theater, and dance to see which one they may enjoy for their entire life.

Electives

You can include many possible electives in middle school. Often, Christian parents include a Bible class. When my children were in middle school, we called it Cozy Couch Time. My two boys and I read from *Josh McDowell's Youth*

Devotions and discussed it. This was fun family bonding time. You can include some character training as well. Make sure children understand what it means to be an upright, moral person with values, as they become adults.

Teaching critical thinking is also important. We used the *Building Thinking Skills* series of books from Critical Thinking Co. They were extremely helpful in guiding my children's thinking skills. Until I picked up the curriculum, I didn't realize you could teach children spatial reasoning; I thought it was something you were born with or without.

Another elective that's often included in middle school is a technology class. Make sure your child has an understanding of how computers work. Keyboarding is also important; you want your child to start typing the right way. When they go on to high school, they should be able to type with speed and accuracy.

Test Preparation

Test taking skills are important, but avoid over-testing. Give a simple yearly assessment that shows how your child is doing each year. It can also help them avoid future testing anxiety because it's a normal part of life, like their annual visit to the doctor. Yearly testing can demonstrate to the child that tests aren't scary — simply a part of life.

Avoid excessive testing in every subject. Instead, focus on the joy of learning, not test preparation.

Sometimes parents come to me concerned about the SAT or ACT test. They know it's important for college admission and want to know whether they should start preparing now, in middle school. The best thing you can do in middle school is teach your child reading, writing, and math, and include penmanship so they are ready for any test.

Provide core, foundational learning your child can build on in future. Now is not the time for test preparation; now is the time for learning.

Boredom Busters for Reluctant Kids

Try to find or create learning games. There are tons of games available online for many different subject areas. Incorporate hands-on learning whenever possible, to make learning a bit easier for them. Your child can learn more than the words on the page, including the meaning and deeper understanding.

Help your child find the relationships between topics. Is there a relationship between what they're learning in art, science, and history? Interdisciplinary studies (e.g. studying history, literature, Bible, and geography together), can be helpful since it reduces boredom. This is why I'm a big fan of a literature-based curriculum, because it provides interdisciplinary studies.

Mix what your child knows and likes with new topics they're learning. This way, they'll understand the material and won't be completely overwhelmed. We used free, downloadable typing software, called Roller Typing. As my children learned how to type, the program occasionally gave them the opportunity to play a short, five-minute video game. The game made it fun for them. Another program we used was Baseball Math. It was a fun way for my children to take what they knew and liked, baseball, and practice figuring out statistics.

Discuss current events around the dinner table. This helps your child gain a better understanding of the real world. When you find out there was a problem with a building and the engineers didn't see it coming, you can discuss it. This is a real world example of the importance of math because mistakes with big repercussions can happen.

Chapter 9

Looking Ahead to High School and Beyond

Learn and Practice High School Record Keeping

The first step towards keeping proper homeschool records is to find out what the law requires. Start by reading your state homeschool law. When you do your research, don't worry about your state's public school law, because it is not what's required of homeschoolers. You can find your state homeschool law here: homehighschoolhelp.com/know-your-state-homeschool-law

One mom contacted me because she was concerned about Ohio law regarding math instruction. We researched together and found out the Ohio state homeschool law said nothing specific about math. Read your state homeschool law carefully and don't get it mixed up with state public school law. Make sure you understand exactly what is required of you now and in high school.

Once you've learned what is required, learn how to keep high school records and practice record keeping. High school record keeping includes creating a transcript, course descriptions, and reading list. Your job in middle school is to learn enough about these three elements of record keeping so you can avoid being fearful of high school. You can learn more about homeschool record keeping in my book, *Setting the Records Straight* on Amazon.

As you start learning about record keeping and practicing it, keep a good pace for you and your learning style. If you learn too much too fast, you will be stressed out, burned out, and hate homeschooling high school. You also don't want to learn too little too late. If you do, you'll get behind, fearful, panic, and eventually quit homeschooling high school.

Make a plan for high school courses. Your plan might include covering French for foreign language and learning a little Latin in middle school so French is easier in high school. Making plans for high school courses can make it easier for you to get the big picture of what you want to cover now.

Earn Early High School Credits

When practicing making a transcript, remember that some of your child's classes in middle school can count as early high school credits. Algebra 1 or higher, high school level science, a whole level of foreign language using a standard high school curriculum, or a high school or college level class can each count as a whole high school credit on your child's transcript.

You can award one high school credit when you complete the textbook or the class. Give a grade and add it to your child's cumulative grade point average (GPA) on the high school transcript.

Research College Financing

College financing can be confusing, so spend time investigating options well in advance. Middle school is the time to think about college for your child's future. Plan challenging high school courses. This is the best way to pay for college. Provide your child with the opportunity to earn merit scholarships and get the best scholarships by planning challenging classes. Math, science, and foreign language are important classes on the road to scholarships.

Whether or not your child earns merit scholarships, consider how you will pay for college. Start doing research on how to get scholarships now, when your children are in middle school. Then you will have a thorough understanding of the ins and outs by the time your child gets to high school.

Although earlier is easier, it's not too late to begin saving for college. Do research on the college 529 Plan. This is considered the best deal right now, but there are state investment plans like the 529. Many of them come into play in middle school so do your research by the time your child is in eighth grade. Learn about the different investment plans available, and try to start setting money aside now. Estimate the financial aid you might receive from colleges. Use the

FAFSA forecaster at: fafsa.ed.gov/FAFSA/app/f4cForm.

You can save a certain percentage of your income and set it aside right off the top. Every time your spouse gets a raise, put the exact amount into your savings. You can also save a specific amount per paycheck, per month, or per year. Consider putting aside your tax refund or Christmas money every year. You can also put aside gifts or inheritances. Consider asking grandparents for money for college savings instead of gifts to add to your child's college savings each birthday.

Research tax deductions and the tax implications of putting money aside for college. Check out whether tax deductions can help you save on taxes each year.

Loans are also an option for college financing. Most financial advisors follow the one-third rule. In general, their advice is to save no more than one-third of the expected cost of college. The rest can come from other sources.

Healthy Middle Schoolers

Make sure your children are healthy. Teach them healthy habits so they become healthy teens and adults. Sleep needs change when your children are in middle school. Ensure they get the sleep they need and go to bed on time so they can wake up on time.

Growth spurts can dramatically affect a child's diet. Provide your child with a healthy diet, even when they experience a growth spurt. When my children went through growth spurts, they were in sports at the same time, so our grocery bill went up dramatically.

Make sure your child gets enough exercise to maintain their physical fitness now and in the future. Teach them about keeping technology boundaries. Explain that technology use can dramatically affect their physical fitness and health. Touch on health because you don't get a second chance to teach them about it.

Finally, make sure you remember that maturity fluctuates. As a registered nurse, I learned that health crises can have the greatest effect on maturity fluctuations. If your child experiences a major health crisis, it can decrease their emotional maturity by two full years.

If your child acts like a seventh grader today, breaks a bone and ends up having surgery, they can act like a fifth grader for weeks. If you do experience a health crisis, expect your child to act much younger than they normally would.

Conclusion

Now is No Time to Panic

Focus on learning in your homeschool and you can't go wrong. When you genuinely care about your child's education, you are taking the necessary steps toward homeschooling successfully through high school graduation.

Homeschooling using any method can be successful. You don't have to change your homeschool style because high school and college are looming. Instead, focus on ensuring your children learn on purpose each day. When your children are in middle school, you can't be "behind." Do your best to educate your children and you can't go wrong!

Spend time in elementary and middle school working through issues as they arise. Parenting doesn't get easier as children get older! Face problems head-on, working through them as they come up so high school will go more smoothly.

Enjoy homeschooling in elementary and middle school as you prepare your child for high school! When you get there, I'm here to help!

Afterword

Who is Lee Binz and What Can She Do for Me?

Number one best-selling homeschool author, Lee Binz is The HomeScholar. Her mission is "helping parents homeschool high school." Lee and her husband, Matt, homeschooled their two boys, Kevin and Alex, from elementary through high school.

Upon graduation, both boys received four-year, full tuition scholarships from their first choice university. This enables Lee to pursue her dream job — helping parents homeschool their children through high school.

On The HomeScholar website, you will find great products for creating homeschool transcripts and comprehensive records to help you amaze and impress colleges.

Find out why Andrew Pudewa, Founder of the Institute for Excellence in Writing says, "Lee Binz knows how to navigate this often confusing and frustrating labyrinth better than anyone."

You can find Lee online at:

HomeHighSchoolHelp.com

If this book has been helpful, could you please take a minute to write us a quick review on Amazon?

Thank you!

Testimonials

We Couldn't Have Done this Without You!

Good news from the Philippines! Our son was accepted at his first-choice school. We are so very grateful for all of the material you made available to us, Lee. How helpful the videos were! I listened to them over and over. Because of your help and advice, I was able to make a wonderful transcript, a beautiful extra-curricular activity sheet, stunning recommendations and prepped for the college exams with your help!

Lee, we could NOT have done this without your help. You calmed my fears that kept me awake at night. You were a true God-send to our lives because of your down-to-earth, effective, clear, practical, and most useful information.

~ Nancy

Calming and Practical Advice

I want to thank you SO MUCH for your help when I was panicking about getting my comprehensive record and transcripts done! In spite of the panic and the work and the time, I am VERY pleased with how they turned out with your guidance. I want to tell you that my son was accepted into every one of the seven schools he applied to, and I am sure the thorough records had quite a bit to do with that.

I certainly know your calming and practical advice and counsel along the way had a huge impact. My son received generous scholarships. I just wanted to be sure to say thank you.

~ Lois

For more information about my **Comprehensive Record Solution** and **Gold Care Club**, go to:

www.ComprehensiveRecordSolution.com
and
www.GoldCareClub.com

Also From The HomeScholar...

- The HomeScholar Guide to College Admission and Scholarships: Homeschool Secrets to Getting Ready, Getting In and Getting Paid (Book and Kindle Book)

- Setting the Records Straight — How to Craft Homeschool Transcripts and Course Descriptions for College Admission and Scholarships (Book and Kindle Book)

- TechnoLogic: How to Set Logical Technology Boundaries and Stop the Zombie Apocalypse

- Finding the Faith to Homeschool High School

- Total Transcript Solution (Online Training, Tools, and Templates)

- Comprehensive Record Solution (Online Training, Tools, and Templates)

- High School Solution (Online Training, Tools, and Templates)

- College Launch Solution (Online Training, Tools, Templates, and Support)

- Gold Care Club (Comprehensive Online Support and Training)

- Silver Training Club (Online Training)

- Parent Training A la Carte (Online Training)

The HomeScholar Coffee Break Books Released or Coming Soon on Kindle and Paperback:

- Delight Directed Learning: Guiding Your Homeschooler Toward Passionate Learning

- Creating Transcripts for Your Unique Child: Help Your Homeschool Graduate Stand Out from the Crowd

- Beyond Academics: Preparation for College and for Life

- Planning High School Courses: Charting the Course Toward High School Graduation

- Graduate Your Homeschooler in Style: Make Your Homeschool Graduation Memorable

- Keys to High School Success: Get Your Homeschool High School Started Right!

- Getting the Most Out of Your Homeschool This Summer: Learning just for the Fun of it!

- Finding a College: A Homeschooler's Guide to Finding a Perfect Fit

- College Scholarships for High School Credit: Learn and Earn With This Two-for-One Strategy!

- College Admission Policies Demystified: Understanding Homeschool Requirements for Getting In

- A Higher Calling: Homeschooling High School for Harried Husbands (by Matt Binz, Mr. HomeScholar)

- Gifted Education Strategies for Every Child: Homeschool Secrets for Success

- College Application Essays: A Primer for Parents

- Creating Homeschool Balance: Find Harmony Between Type A and Type Zzz...

- Homeschooling the Holidays: Sanity Saving Strategies and Gift Giving Ideas

- Your Goals this Year: A Year by Year Guide to Homeschooling High School

- Making the Grades: A Grouch-Free Guide to Homeschool Grading

- High School Testing: Knowledge That Saves Money

- Getting the BIG Scholarships: Learn Expert Secrets for Winning College Cash!

- Easy English for Simple Homeschooling: How to Teach, Assess and Document High School English

- Scheduling — The Secret to Homeschool Sanity: Plan You Way Back to Mental Health

- Junior Year is the Key to High School Success: How to Unlock the Gate to Graduation and Beyond

- Upper Echelon Education: How to Gain Admission to Elite Universities

- How to Homeschool College: Save Time, Reduce Stress and Eliminate Debt

- Homeschool Curriculum That's Effective and Fun: Avoid the Crummy Curriculum Hall of Shame!

- Comprehensive Homeschool Records: Put Your Best Foot Forward to Win College Admission and Scholarships

- Options After High School: Steps to Success for College or Career

- How to Homeschool 9th and 10th Grades: Simple Steps for Starting Strong!

- Senior Year Step-by-Step: Simple Instructions for Busy Homeschool Parents

- How to Homeschool Independently: Do-it-Yourself Secrets to Rekindle the Love of Learning

- High School Math The Easy Way: Simple Strategies for Homeschool Parents in Over Their Heads

- Homeschooling Middle School with Powerful Purpose: How to Successfully Navigate 6th through 8th Grades

- Simple Science for Homeschooling High School: Because Teaching Science isn't Rocket Science!

- How to Be Your Child's Best College Coach: Strategies for Success Using Teens You'll Find Lying Around the House

- Teen Tips for College and Career Success: Learn Why 10 C's are Better Than All A's or APs

Would you like to be notified when we offer the next *Coffee Break Books* for FREE during our Kindle promotion days? If so, leave your name and email below and we will send you a reminder.

HomeHighSchoolHelp.com/
freekindlebook

Visit my Amazon Author Page!

amazon.com/author/leebinz

Made in the USA
Columbia, SC
24 January 2022